Presented to:

From:

COMMENCE!

Concise Advice for the
Next Adventure of Life

Jeff Lovejoy

A LeaderQuips™ Publication

Commence! Concise Advice for the Next Adventure of Life
First Edition, 2024
Copyright © 2024 by Jeff Lovejoy

A LeaderQuips™ Publication

To order additional books:
www.CommenceBook.com
www.LeaderQuips.com
www.Amazon.com

ISBN: 978-1-952943-30-0

Editorial and Book Packaging: Inspira Literary Solutions

Printed in the USA

Table of Contents

Introduction

The title of this book came from the realization that my teenage daughter was approaching her final year of high school. The conclusion of her studies would culminate in an event that many call "Graduation," which is also commonly referred to as "Commencement." I found it to be quizzical that these two words were interchangeable, although they have very different meanings. The term "Graduation" seems to focus backward, celebrating the completion of something significant, accomplishment of a goal, the closing of a chapter, whereas "Commencement" looks forward, focusing on the excitement and challenge of what lies ahead, commanding us to "get going." I loved the idea of turning the concepts in this book into "action verbs" rather than just static concept "nouns."

You may notice that many of the concepts appear to compete with one another. Let's frame this differently and call it "balance." Rarely is anything either 100 percent positive or 100 percent negative, good or bad. Rather, life requires a blend of approaches, in the right amounts and with appropriate timing.

Do your best to become a "student of life," and never stop learning. Beyond that, the best way to lock in your own learning is to teach it to someone else. So, don't keep all of your wisdom to yourself!

As you read and re-read and ruminate on the concepts in this book, think of them as a call to action, not just "neat ideas." You can choose to live life from the passenger seat, or the back seat, or maybe even from the side-lines . . . but that's not how you're designed. You were created to embrace experiences, conquer challenges, learn, grow, serve, enjoy, and so much more. But you will never become the person you can be, or live the life you desire, by sitting still.

Get up, get going . . . COMMENCE!

MIND

Dream Massively

Before you can achieve it, you must first believe it. Believe that you have limitless potential . . . let your hopes and dreams run wild without boundaries.

Not sure how to achieve your dreams? Even better! Scarce resources simply require an abundance of creativity. If you cannot see something, you'll never be something. Envision a big, bold, bright future for yourself. **Dream massively.**

Observe Everything

Decisions have consequences, both positive and negative. We learn from our own decisions, and we can also learn by observing the outcomes of the decisions of others. "When the student is ready, the teacher will appear," as the saying goes.

If we simply tune in and pay attention, opportunities to learn will be all around us all the time. Looking around and paying attention is an easy way to leverage learning. **Observe everything.**

Take Risks

Anyone who never takes a risk will never taste a reward. Not all risks are good risks, of course. Jumping into dark water without knowledge of what's below? That's just reckless. But Helen Keller expressed it beautifully when she said, "Life is either a daring adventure, or nothing." Do your research, assess the dangers, seek wise counsel . . . and then act.

Opportunity does exist, but rarely, if ever, does it demand your attention. Jump smartly. **Take risks.**

Read Voraciously

Information is continuously expanding and increasingly available. Yet many people refuse to read unless it's required.

Books come in all shapes and sizes and lengths and languages, and they contain concepts beyond what you've already learned. Expansive thinkers love to read because they love to learn. **Read voraciously.**

Learn Forever

Some people might determine "old age" by the number of candles on their birthday cake, the appearance of their body, or the condition of their mind. But all these metrics are correlational, not causal. The one thing that truly makes a person old is when they stop learning and growing and start shrinking and settling for "good enough." The world is accelerating at an ever-increasing pace, and it's our job to keep up and keep learning.

Education may be a requirement, but learning is a luxury. **Learn forever.**

Keep Calm

As we develop our skills, we collect new capabilities that allow us to solve bigger and bigger problems with less and less effort. Situations that would have derailed you a few years ago barely feel like a speed bump anymore. As your competence grows, so will your confidence, and so will your composure.

"Courage under fire" is a crucial skill for a battlefield leader, and there are days when life may feel a bit like a battlefield. Clear thinking solves problems. Cool heads prevail. **Keep calm.**

Be Careful

Every parent wants to see their children live long enough to become thriving adults. So, "Don't play in traffic," and, "Don't run with scissors," are some maxims commonly uttered. But being careful goes far beyond that. It means developing an awareness for hidden dangers, the landmines of life. Learning to be ever-vigilant means developing a healthy skepticism and approaching new situations with an appropriate level of caution.

Don't let fear stop you from taking action, but trust your gut to keep you safe from harm. **Be careful.**

Get Angry

To any given stimulus, there is a broad spectrum of potential responses. Some people never seem to get upset by anything. Maybe nothing really matters enough to make them angry. We might call them apathetic. On the other end of the spectrum are those who get upset by even the tiniest of slights. They are emotional, unpredictable, and sometimes even volatile. The challenge here is for you to determine the things you will stand up for. Bullying, injustice, bigotry, aggression, oppression . . . these are things that we cannot afford to ignore.

The only requirement for evil to prevail is for good people to do nothing. **Get angry.**

Say Yes

There is a really fun movie, titled *Yes Man*, with Jim Carrey. When he makes a commitment to say "Yes" to every opportunity, his otherwise boring, downtrodden life takes a massive turn toward adventure and excitement. Every time you stretch yourself and say "Yes" to something, it requires courage to follow through on the commitment. And, once you've done it, you've now added a new capability to your toolbox of experiences.

Challenge yourself to try new things, especially things that make you uncomfortable. **Say yes.**

Say No

If you are the type of person who tends to prioritize others' needs ahead of your own, this one is for you. You may not want to let other people down, or maybe you believe you can always find a way to squeeze "one more thing" onto the list. This can leave you stretched too thin and stressed too often. Learning to say "No" is a sign of strength, not weakness.

Prioritizing your own well-being is required for mental, physical, and emotional health.Remember to reserve some energy for yourself. **Say no.**

Speak Up

Sometimes you may not feel like your thoughts are worth sharing. Share them anyway. You may not feel like it is "your place" to point out a problem or an injustice. Call it out anyway. Maybe you don't think you're ready to go public with an unpolished idea. Publish it anyway. Don't shrink away from an opportunity to let your voice be heard. Embrace altruism. Stand and deliver.

See something? Say something. **Speak up.**

Shut Up

Some people seem to believe we want to hear every thought that hits their brain. News flash . . . we don't! Social media platforms have made it easy for anyone to share pretty much anything, with a lot of people, whether it is valuable or not. There is wisdom in discretion; there is wisdom in silence.

Pay attention to the ratio of your contributions relative to the number of people within earshot. Contribute proportionately, and don't overshare. **Shut up.**

Stand Up

There are moments in our lives when we are faced with something that demands we take action. To shrink away from such responsibility would be to essentially promote a negative outcome . . . thus, we are compelled to act. The seeds of regret are most often planted in the soil of apathy and inaction.

Find your strength, face your fear. **Stand up.**

Sit Down

For action-oriented people, being "DIY minded" is a way of life. We may tend to think we can do something better or faster than someone else, so we "just do it." But, when we keep doing things ourselves, we block others from learning, failing, and growing.

Learn to "let go and let grow." **Sit down.**

BODY

Eat Healthy

Years ago I picked up a brochure that touted the "Three Pillars of Health": strength, endurance, and flexibility. But it was missing a key ingredient: nutrition. "Nothing tastes as good as healthy feels" is a great way to think about this. If we eat like chumps, how can we possibly expect to perform like champions?

Nutrition experts don't always agree on what perfect nutrition looks like, but they typically agree on what "bad" looks like. Do your research, ask your doctor, talk to a nutrition expert. Feed your body what it needs . . . it will thank you. **Eat healthy.**

Exercise Regularly

Our bodies are simply miraculous, capable of incredible things . . . if we take care of them. Given that we have these amazing vehicles that are designed to run, jump, climb, lift, and swim, why do we crave comfort so much? We spend small fortunes on cushy, soft, pillow-covered furniture so we can sit comfortably and stare at a box watching other people run, jump, climb, lift, and swim. Many of the most common health problems people face today are a result of poor nutrition, a lack of movement, or both. So, get up off the couch and get moving! You can be a marathoner, or you can take a walk around the block. You can go to the gym, or you can drop to the floor and do some pushups.

Whatever you choose to do, just do something— and keep doing it. **Exercise regularly.**

Acknowledge Habits

Thoughts create actions and actions create habits. We all have them. Some habits work well for us and lift us up, while others undermine us and drag us down. The trick is to first recognize and acknowledge our habits, and then to assess whether or not they are helping or hurting us.

We can't do anything about improving our habits until we first recognize and understand them. **Acknowledge habits.**

Adjust Habits

Over time, habits determine our results, which determine our future, and ultimately our life and legacy. Habits determine the trajectory of life. Their momentum is undeniable. But what if you have bad habits today? Are you doomed? No way! Habits take weeks or even years to form, so they need to be given a similar runway to be changed.

Determine the triggers that cause your bad habits, work on reprogramming what the trigger means, and the habit will fade. Then, work on replacing the old or bad habit with a new or better one. **Adjust habits.**

SPIRIT

Pray Quietly

Healthy relationships require trust, transparency, and consistent communication. A relationship with God is no different. He wants to know you, He wants to have a relationship with you, He wants to hear from you. We are members of a community, and public worship is a common part of membership. However, the best connections are one on one, candid, personal, and private.

God wants to know you. Nurture your relationship with Him. **Pray quietly.**

Trust God

If you believe God exists, then trust Him. Assuming you are human, living on this planet among other humans, then you know people will disappoint you. Family, friends, siblings, lovers . . . they will all let you down. Some will break their promises; others will break your heart. Do not turn away from people, but rather, turn toward God.

God, by whatever name He is called, is worthy of your trust, and He will never betray you. **Trust God.**

Exhibit Wisdom

Knowledge is great, but it is only part of the picture. Life requires that we make decisions and take action.

Wisdom is gained from actions and experiences; it is knowledge applied. Thoughts manifest into actions, actions become habits, and habits create destiny. Beginning with your thoughts, take control of your destiny by applying what you've learned. **Exhibit wisdom.**

Live Gratefully

Approaching life as though the world owes you something is a ticket to depression. An attitude of entitlement tends to repel other people. Be grateful for everything, expect nothing, and be pleasantly surprised when things come your way. Replace the phrase "have to" with "get to," and be amazed at how your outlook improves.

Happy people are grateful people, and grateful people are happy people. **Live gratefully.**

Welcome Adversity

If you're like most people, you probably succeed more than you fail. It's actually pretty easy to lower the bar, not challenge yourself, only do what you're already good at, and avoid uncomfortable situations. That's complacency. But that's not where growth happens. That's not where we feel most alive.

Seek discomfort: stretch beyond your limits, and say "Yes" when you have no idea how you're going to do something. Challenge demands courage; adversity makes us better, stronger, smarter.

The boring bus is for adversity avoiders. Buy a ticket on the adventure bus instead. **Welcome adversity.**

Seek Balance

The phrase "crazy busy" seems like the new badge of honor for high achievers, but whom are we trying to impress? Step out of yourself from time to time and take stock of the diverse aspects of your life. A friend introduced me to the "Six Fs" years ago: Faith, Family, Friends, Fitness, Finance, Fun. Make investments in each "F," and pay attention to those where you may be under-indexed and need to make some adjustments.

Be a whole person. **Seek balance.**

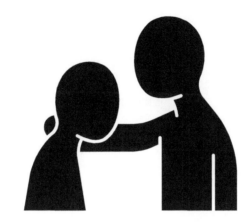

Show Compassion

If you've ever been around someone who didn't "meet the standard," they're likely to be pretty down about it. They didn't pass the test, they didn't get the job, they didn't meet the deadline . . . they failed. During those moments, they don't need you to point out their shortcomings. They need your compassion.

Even if a failure is 100 percent someone's own fault, that fact doesn't make it any less painful. What they need in that moment isn't judgment or coaching . . . it's a friend with a listening heart. **Show compassion.**

Leave Footprints

Have you ever been the only person out in nature? An early morning stroll on the beach, a sunrise hike on an unpopular trail, a rainy boat ride when you're the only one up on deck and everyone else is huddled below? These are rare opportunities to really get in touch with nature, with yourself, with the universe, and with God.

Don't wait. Be bold, be independent: go alone. You'll be amazed how great it can feel for your footprints to be the only ones you see. **Leave footprints.**

RELATIONSHIPS

Love People

Love is the most powerful force in the universe. It is so much more than a transient feeling that happens by chance. In reality, love is an action verb that requires your intentional participation. Love demands that you put aside your own selfish desires and put another person first.

Take control of your love life. Go on the offensive and become an instrument of caring, healing, and positive affirmation. **Love people.**

Forgive Hurts

Sometimes, we get hurt. Physical pain is difficult, but verbal, social, and emotional pain stings more and lasts longer than the slice of a knife blade. Sometimes, those hurts are inflicted by those closest to us, and sometimes, it happens over and over and over.

"Hurt people often hurt people," but retaliate with compassion. Fight back with love. **Forgive hurts.**

Call Mom

Moms are awesome. They loved you enough to want you, to have you, and then to take care of you and protect you. During the early years, we're inseparable from Mom. So why then, is it so easy to move away and forget to call or visit? Mom will always be your biggest champion and your loudest cheerleader . . . and she'll even bring snacks and brag about you from the sidelines.

Don't forget about your biggest fan. **Call Mom.**

Call Dad

Dads are awesome, too. They taught you how to practice and how to play; they taught you how to fix broken stuff and take better care of it so it doesn't break again. They brag about you to their buddies, even if they reprimand you. Just like moms, they love you in their own way. Moms tend to be more concerned about protecting you from pain, while dads tend to focus on preparing you to face the world and win.

Don't be fooled by the "tough guy" exterior. Underneath it all, Dad can be melted with a hug, a card, or even a quick phone call. **Call Dad.**

Ask Curiously

Great conversations are fueled by great questions.
Our questions reflect our level of interest.

Genuine curiosity is the highest level of interest and the catalyst for the
very best questions. Set aside personal bias, increase your level of interest,
ask great questions, and then be quiet and listen. **Ask curiously.**

Listen Intently

Listening is a skill that feels like it's on the verge of extinction. The ability to ask a meaningful question, to be genuinely curious about the answer, and to patiently await the response is more valuable than a gemstone.

Be rare, be valuable, be curious: ask questions . . .
and don't interrupt. **Listen intently.**

Cut Cleanly

There will be people in your life who will be bad for you. Sure, they might be fun to hang with, and they might even be very close to you and know your secrets. But when you know in your heart that you'd be better off without them in your life, you need to take the initiative and cut them off. It may seem harsh . . . but your reputation and your future are at stake.

Wrong crowd = wrong future. Don't drag it out. **Cut cleanly.**

Hug Warmly

Humans were not designed to be independent organisms. We need each other, we crave connections, we require relationships. Numerous studies have proven that infants who aren't held regularly do not develop as quickly as those who are. Later in life, they often struggle with attachment issues. Hugs are a free and simple means of expressing care for one another. Be the person who hugs first, and challenge yourself to hold on for two seconds longer than you normally would. Use both arms and give a little sigh of "umph" to signal your enjoyment of knowing the other person.

Make it part of your personal brand to become
a great hugger. **Hug warmly.**

Encourage Proactively

We are around people all the time who may be struggling in silence, privately discouraged. Whether it's out of pride or privacy, they won't ever ask for encouragement or share their struggles. Go on the attack!

Pretend everyone you meet is wearing a T-shirt with the words "Encourage Me!" on it. Even if they don't need the encouragement, you'll both feel elevated anyway. **Encourage proactively.**

Keep Secrets

When we are entrusted with private, confidential information, it is our duty to keep that confidence. Friendships fail, marriages end, companies collapse, and everyone gets hurt when trust is broken. Whatever reason you may feel justifies sharing a secret . . . it doesn't.

There is always a painful price for betrayal. **Keep secrets.**

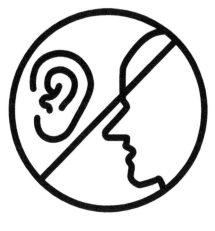

Quell Gossip

Some people seem compelled to spread "news" about others. Maybe it's their way of feeling important or wanting to be perceived as being "in the know." Whatever the reason, it's wrong. Unless it is a compliment, the only people being talked about in a conversation should be the people actually present in that conversation.

Become known as the kind of person who won't tolerate gossip. Share only praise and good news about others. **Quell gossip.**

MONEY

Manage Money

Money is a means of assessing and transacting economic value—nothing more, nothing less. Unfortunately, money carries with it so much stigma and status that it has almost become a deity.

Don't worship money, but do respect it, manage it closely, and discipline yourself to save some of it. Learn to suppress excess wants and live in a manner that allows you to always have some left over. "Save" might be a four-letter word, but "poor" is a worse one. **Manage money.**

Save Deliberately

Putting aside at least 10 percent of whatever you earn, before doing anything else, is called "paying yourself first." Yes, there will always be big expenses like rent, food, gas, insurance, utilities, etc. That is why it becomes even more important to build a budget and make sure that budget includes savings as the top line item.

If you don't put savings at the top of the list, there will never be enough left over at the bottom of the list. **Save deliberately.**

Spend Frugally

Discipline yourself to spend less than you earn. There will always be things we want yet cannot afford. Sadly, there will even be times we cannot afford what we need. Keep your wants under control and avoid overspending, even on needs.

Prices for many things can fluctuate widely depending on the time, location, and marketplace supply and demand. Research upcoming expenses and refuse to overpay. **Spend frugally.**

Give Generously

It is foolish to think we ever really "own" anything.
Everything is really just on loan to us.

Our time, our energy, our knowledge, our money, our love, and
even our lives will all be taken away someday. We are merely
temporary stewards of these gifts, and we will benefit ourselves
and others most by sharing them easily. Scarcity thinking tightens
our grips, but abundant thinking opens our hands. "Givers get" is a
common maxim, but we should never expect anything in return.
Every door will open for a generous heart. **Give generously.**

Donate Decisively

The act of donating makes you feel great about yourself, and I can't recall anyone ever expressing regret about helping someone else. People and organizations "in need" are all around us, all the time, asking for assistance. However, with limited resources, we can't help everyone. So "tune in" to your heart, listen to what speaks to you, and invest in those efforts. The principle is simple, "Your heart will follow your money, so make your money follow you heart." **Donate decisively.**

Delay Gratification

Babies cry because they want something . . . right now. Food, sleep, a fresh diaper . . . whatever it is, their brains can't embrace the concept of waiting. Some adults still act like babies. Maybe they don't cry, but they also can't wait. Don't like my car? Get a new one! See an advertisement? Go shopping! Money in my pocket? Spend it! Learning to defer our desires is a crucial milestone on the road to maturity.

The road to success is paved with self-discipline. **Delay gratification.**

Avoid Debt

Believing in yourself and having a bright outlook on your future are excellent ways to approach life. But being overly optimistic about your financial future can lead to debt, and debt can become a prison.

If you borrow from tomorrow to pay for today, you'll end up carrying an emotional burden in addition to the financial burden. **Avoid debt.**

Invest Wisely

There are many aspects of life that exist on the spectrum of risk versus reward, but few are as widely measured and debated as investing your money. Everyone has a "favorite stock" or a "great deal" to tell you about, but ask them about their losses and most will change the subject or blame someone else. Investing is partly about making money, but mostly about accepting the responsibility that goes with the risk.

Inspect before you invest. Only buy into what you truly understand. **Invest wisely.**

Budget Thoughtfully

A budget is nothing more than spending your money on paper before you have it. Some people might say budgets are restrictive, but they are just the opposite. Knowing where your money will go gives you the power to control it. Not knowing where your money goes—and running out of it—means money has control over you.

Make a plan to "spend your money on paper" before you have it, and you'll have tremendous peace of mind. **Budget thoughtfully.**

RECREATION

Explore Widely

Far too many people live small lives in small containers thinking small thoughts . . . until they die and get buried in even smaller containers with no thoughts. Don't die having never really lived.

There are billions of people inhabiting hundreds of countries with thousands of cultures, communities, and cuisines, all available for you to experience if you will simply begin by saying, "Let's go." **Explore widely.**

Be Spontaneous

Do you know someone who doesn't do anything without first making a plan? They are great to have around because they can help create budgets, allocate time, even predict problems. But don't they just get on your nerves sometimes? Don't you just wish that they would "leap before they look" even once?

Some of the best memories are created by serendipity: seemingly random opportunities that arise suddenly and expire immediately. When someone offers, "Hey, c'mon, let's go," just go. **Be spontaneous.**

Sing Joyfully

Music in its many forms has been around since the first human beings. Why? Because music touches our hearts and awakens our souls far more than words alone. If you have a great singing voice, share it with others to lift their spirits. If you don't have a great singing voice, sing anyway to lift your own spirit. Even sad songs can bring tears of joy.

Ignore critics . . . sing songs that make your heart leap and your spirit soar. **Sing joyfully.**

Be Silly

For those among us who place a heavy emphasis on productivity and results, the idea of goofiness is practically illegal: "There's no time for silliness, we have stuff to do." Maybe that's true. But don't suck all the air out of the room. Don't be a killjoy. It is possible, you know, to get a lot done and still have some fun. Make a funny face, tell an embarrassing story about yourself, or play a quick round of rock, paper, scissors to see who has to go get lunch.

Taking a little break every once in a while isn't just about being goofy: it helps you connect with others and create camaraderie. Crack a smile—it won't kill you! **Be silly.**

Be Serious

On the flip side of silly is the need to focus, be productive, and get the job done. The class clown is often the person everyone likes to hang out with, but they are not the person you call when you have a flat tire or need a critical eye to review your work. When you want something done well and on time, you call a busy person. You call your driven, focused, serious friend.

If you want to be the "trusted advisor," the person people call in a pinch, you need a clear head and focused attention. **Be serious.**

65

Take Photos

The older we get, the faster it seems time flies by. Birthday parties, weekends with friends, even the time the car broke down and it turned into an epic adventure . . . those are special memories that often get buried and forgotten. But they can be brought back to full splendor in our memory with a single photo.

Don't let picture taking derail the moment, but do try to remember to take a photo or two so you can relive that special moment anytime you want. **Take photos.**

PRODUCTIVITY

Write Goals

Everyone has something they want to achieve. Some people chase lofty pursuits that will stretch them beyond their limits, and others may simply seek to get through the day. Depending on your interests and ambitions, your goals will be very different from most everyone else's. That's totally acceptable, but be intentional about your goals. Don't just think them; write them down to burn them into your subconscious.

Seek to improve, inspect what you expect, and enjoy the journey. **Write goals.**

Uphold Standards

Many aspects of our lives are regularly measured: our height, weight, test grades, attendance, etc. Most of the time, such measurements are used simply to assign comparative value. Sometimes, though, when it really matters, there is an established standard. Not meeting that standard could cause serious consequences.

One of my mentors explained it succinctly: "You don't get what you expect, you get what you tolerate." Where these standards exist, they do so for a reason, and should be upheld. When it really matters, don't tolerate anything less. Don't waiver. **Uphold standards.**

Guard Time

Yesterday is gone forever and tomorrow is never guaranteed. The "precious present" is the only clay with which we get to mold our lives. Do you waste time in activities that drain your energy or dull your mind? Or spend time with people who bring you down and projects that weaken your spirit? View your time as you would a pile of diamonds, considering each hour a rare gem and a chance to invest in something worthwhile and accretive to your life.

Time is your treasure. **Guard time.**

Waste Time

Do you know anyone who has a hard time letting loose, who is practically incapable of relaxation? Certainly, we need to invest most of our time wisely, but we won't be fully human unless we are also able to be gentle with ourselves occasionally. Being intensely serious and productive for long periods can be both exhilarating and exhausting.

From time to time, give yourself permission to do nothing. **Waste time.**

Review Results

Achievement-oriented people have an innate tendency to focus on "what's next"—extensive lists of tasks to be done, projects to finish, deadlines to meet, gaps to close.. The feeling of "never enough" can be overwhelming. Learn to take a break periodically, and "measure backwards." Acknowledge and celebrate how far you've already come, the milestones you've met, the higher levels you've attained.

We can't live in the past, but when our tank is running low, looking back at our gains can become the jet fuel to propel us forward. **Review results.**

Persist Politely

Our society has evolved so much in the last 100 years, and especially in the last 10, that almost anything we need or want can be had with minimal effort. This on-demand availability has, for some, eroded their drive, determination and dedication. But a successful life is not typically an easy one. Those who succeed in any field have an inner "why" that drives them. It forces them to push through obstacles and work with others, not against them, to charge forward.

No one succeeds alone in this world, and pushing for what we want often attracts likeminded people. So reinforce your resolve, recruit friends, and overcome obstacles. **Persist politely.**

Respond Promptly

Some societal norms feel like they are on life support—not quite dead yet, but not really thriving anymore, either. One such norm is the RSVP. When we're unsure of changing plans or waiting for a better offer, there is a tendency to delay our reply to invitations. This can apply to phone calls and texts, too. Someone reaches out to us and, whether because of busyness or forgetfulness, we neglect to respond. Frankly, it's disrespectful.

When someone reaches out and seeks a reply, don't leave them hanging. **Respond promptly.**

Wait Patiently

In an increasingly fast-paced, digital world, it feels as though our brains are being rewired and our internal clocks recalibrated into ever-smaller units of time. Waiting more than a few minutes in line can feel like an eternity. Not getting an immediate text back makes us wonder if the recipient has their notifications turned off. Everyone sitting in a doctor's waiting room is scrolling incessantly on their phone. Impatience seems like an epidemic.

Learn to relax in the moment, look around, let your mind wander, and enjoy the inactivity. **Wait patiently.**

Arrive Promptly

Many sports enthusiasts are familiar with the concept of "Lombardi Time." Famously, Vince was known for the standard that "Fifteen minutes early is on-time, on-time is late, and late is unacceptable." Increasing demands on our time can leave us overscheduled and habitually behind. However, keep in mind that being on time is an important way to show respect for one another, and for ourselves.

Sometimes, being late simply cannot be helped. But if you regularly run behind . . . make changes. Create a cushion in your calendar. Plan better, leave earlier. **Arrive promptly.**

Leave Promptly

Have you ever hosted a party that lasted a little too long? Ever had that friend who was the last one to leave, not wanting the good times to end? Some people are simply clueless, while others may be innately selfish and not really care about how other people feel. Don't be "that person" who overstays their welcome.

Be respectful, read the room, and pay attention to the energy level of your hosts and fellow guests. **Leave promptly.**

Serve Boldly

Somewhere along the way, the word "servant" seems to have taken on a rather undesirable meaning. In some socio-cultural settings, being of service is synonymous with being "lesser than," subservient, or maybe even unworthy. Unfortunately, these sorts of interpretations can prevent us from understanding the intrinsic power that is ignited by a sincere desire to serve. What a beautiful world it would be if we all had hearts that sought to "out-serve" one another.

Take the bold step to serve first, serve well, and expect nothing in return. **Serve boldly.**

Lead Humbly

Leadership is a complex topic. Find any book on the subject and you're likely to discover anywhere from five to 25 (or more) components. One of the most commonly misunderstood aspects of leadership is that of humility. Leading well isn't about having the biggest title or the loudest voice. It typically involves caring the most and showing regard for others' needs before your own.

Don't let positional power go to your head. **Lead humbly.**

Acknowledgments

This book is dedicated to the vast array of relationships and experiences that have shaped me into the person I've become . . . so far.

To call out just a few of the many special people who have had the greatest impact on my life, I'll begin with my parents, Jay and Lee Lovejoy, whom I find myself emulating more and more every day.

Next, my brother Vince, who helped to toughen me up as only a big brother can do, and we grow closer with each passing year. Next, Jana, my beloved wife of 20 years (as of April, 2024) who has taught me what real love looks like, and who has remained my champion through myriad foibles, fumbles and failures. Next, our amazing daughter Shelby, for whom this work was initially conceived and compiled.

From there, I'll acknowledge the diverse cast of friends and mentors who have either been a cheerleader or coach or both, as this book and my life have evolved. Those dear friends are Jennifer Bryarly, Marco Thornton, Serges Himbaza, Bob Sanders, Denny Hanrahan, Jim Suss, Link Moore, Dirk Hansen, Pablo Romera, Bob Rayes, Joel Goehner, Joel Sullivan, Dana Shute, and posthumously, Don Hillenmeyer, Wade Townsley, and Dr. Harold Mc Alindon.

Next, Arlyn Lawrence and her fantastic team at Inspira Literary Solutions, without whom this project would never have been completed.

Finally, I am most eternally grateful for the sacrifice of my personal Lord and Savior, Jesus Christ.

About the Author

Jeff Lovejoy has been a student of leadership for over 25 years and a collector of ideas and experiences his entire life. The concepts in this book are a reflection of hundreds of books read and thousands of hours invested in personal growth and development. Jeff enjoys working, learning, exploring, and spending time with his wife and daughter from their home in Dallas, Texas.

Jeff can be reached at www.LeaderQuips.com

Find Jeff on Youtube

Find Jeff on LinkedIn

9 781952 943300